THE LITTLE BOOK OF
CHELSEA

THIRD EDITION

Unofficial and unauthorised

EDITED BY
CLIVE BATTY

CARLTON
BOOKS

First published by Carlton Books in 2003
Reprinted with updates in 2006, 2007
Second edition 2010
Third edition 2014

Carlton Books Limited
20 Mortimer Street
London W1T 3JW

This book is not an officially licensed product of
Chelsea Football Club

A CIP catalogue record of this book is available from the British Library.

ISBN 978-1-78097-588-7

Printed in Dubai

CONTENTS

INTRODUCTION

Forget the *Mousetrap*, the longest-running, most dramatic
show in London is staged at Stamford Bridge. Reviews
have been mixed over the years, but for jaw-dropping plot
twists the multi-billion-pound production that is 'The Blues'
simply can't be topped. Ecstatic highs, depth-plumbing
lows, silverware and scandal, with an all-star cast drawn
from the four corners of the globe, this show has the lot.

In this great collection of quotes, players, fans and
managers reveal why, for them, Blue really is the colour.
From the glory of the 1955 title and the glamour days of
the 1970s, to the 15 major trophies the Blues have won
since 1997 and the Roman Abramovich era, there are
soundbites to satisfy every Chelsea fan. Peter Osgood,
Terry Venables, Dennis Wise, Ken Bates, Frank Lampard
and John Terry are all featured along with a host of
great managers, from Gianluca Vialli and Carlo
Ancelotti to Felipe Scolari and, of course, the
incomparable Jose Mourinho.

Chelsea is London's undisputed glamour club – no
wonder then that so many people have so much to
say about it.

CHAPTER 1

WE LOVE CHELSEA

" Life is never dull at Stamford Bridge. **"**

KEN BATES

" Becoming a Chelsea director was one of the most marvellous things that has happened in my life. **"**

LORD ATTENBOROUGH

"We always win if Concorde flies over the Bridge while we're playing.**"**

FRANCIS GLIBBERY

Chelsea programme photographer, October 1999

❝Of all the roles Chelsea are expected to fulfil – highest ticket prices in the league, snazziest restaurant, chairman with the most voluminous beard – winning the title is not one of them. **❞**

JIM WHITE

writer and Manchester United fan, October 1998

❝Modern-day newspapers would have had a field day just following Chelsea around. We wouldn't have been off the front or back pages.**❞**

DAVID WEBB

on the 70s side, November 2000

❝Chelsea FC will never lose its identity. Chelsea will be Chelsea for always – and at Stamford Bridge. **❞**

BRIAN MEARS

Chelsea chairman at a time of financial crisis, April 1977

> **"**Last Thursday we received a letter, dated next Monday, complaining about appalling language in the Shed at today's match against Everton. You have been warned!**"**

KEN BATES

September 1991

❝Quite frankly there are some players here who are simply not good enough.**❞**

KEN BATES

May 1983

❝People still come up to me and say thanks for some fantastic memories. That really brings home that you've played a part in this club's great history. It really means something special. **❞**

KERRY DIXON

" I've been coming to Chelsea for 55 years and it's one of the joys of my life. No matter what concerns I have about work or other matters, for that hour and a half watching out there, it's just magic. I absolutely love it. **"**

LORD ATTENBOROUGH

"Matthew was always bubbly. He loved being amongst us. That's the way he'd want to be remembered, I reckon. A bubbly, nice, respected Chelsea supporter.**"**

DENNIS WISE

pays tribute to Matthew Harding, October 1996

"Matthew was one of us. In many ways he was like one of the players. There was always a warm heart there for him and from him.**"**

RUUD GULLIT

October 1996

❝You should never go back in life. You don't see many people out with their ex-wives, do you?**❞**

KEN BATES

ruling out a Bridge return for Dennis Wise, September 2002

“I wanted to build an exciting new Chelsea, providing such entertainment that the players got a standing ovation from the fans even if they lost.**”**

KEN BATES

outlines his football vision, May 1984

"The day I walked through the door I just thought what a magnificent ground, magnificent stadium, fantastic name, and a tremendous location. Why isn't this club bigger than Arsenal and Spurs?**"**

KEN BATES

July 1977

"When my team looked into clubs with the best possible fundamentals and prospects, Chelsea really did come first. The ground, the location, the Champions League qualification, the staff and players and fan support were, and remain, a wonderful foundation.**"**

ROMAN ABRAMOVICH

August 2003

> **"** He might be a billionaire but he is already regarded as one of us – a Chelsea, or Chelski, Boy. **"**

KEN BATES

on Roman Abramovich, August 2003

"I don't want to change what works. I just want to help take what we have at Stamford Bridge to the next level. And I want us all to work hard and have a lot of fun doing it.**"**

ROMAN ABRAMOVICH

August 2003

"I don't seek publicity, it seeks me."

KEN BATES

❝I had one agent phoning up saying,
'I have the honour of representing one of the
world's greatest players, he needs no
introduction.' I said, 'You're right, I don't want
to meet him.' **❞**

KEN BATES

keeps his chequebook shut, summer 2002

" Without our fantastic supporters, there would not be a Chelsea Football Club and we will never forget that. In the future, we hope to bring you more joy than you have experienced in the last hundred years. **"**

ROMAN ABRAMOVICH

2005

"By 2014 we want to be internationally recognised as the No. 1 club. It's a very ballsy vision but one that has captured the interest of the owner.**"**

PETER KENYON

reveals the extent of Chelsea's ambition, November 2006

CHAPTER 2

HEROES OF THE SHIRT

"I didn't get that worked-up in the dressing room. Instead, I used to read the programme to see who I had to kick that week.**"**

RON "CHOPPER" HARRIS

" Tommy Docherty and Ron 'Chopper' Harris invented soccer violence. It's when they retired that it spread to the terraces. **"**

PETER OSGOOD

Peter Osgood has never been replaced since the day Chelsea sold him.

ALAN HUDSON

January 2001

❝I like to think that, apart from being a bit of a butcher, I've something else to offer.**❞**

RON HARRIS

1979

❝I'm a goalkeeper, so I expected
the outfield players to gang up on me
at some point. **❞**

PETER BONETTI

after being voted off a "footballers' special" edition of
The Weakest Link

❝I feel I am coming to a club where I have a genuine chance of winning something. **❞**

CLIVE WILSON

on joining Chelsea in August 1987. Nine months later the Blues were relegated again

"Leading Chelsea back to the First Division is the biggest thrill of my life.**"**

RAY WILKINS

May 1977

❝The worst crowd trouble I saw was down at Millwall. In the warm-up, there were people coming out of the crowd with meat-hooks in their heads. I think that's the only time I've been frightened in a game.❞

IAN BRITTON

recalls a terrifying trip to The Den in 1976

❝ Kevin Keegan turned to me on the pitch and said, 'You've got big problems here.' I wasn't going to argue with him. By that time, 1980–81, there were a lot of petty divisions among the players. **❞**

JOHN BUMSTEAD

March 2002

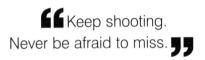

Keep shooting.
Never be afraid to miss.

KERRY DIXON

outlines his goal-scoring philosophy, February 1985

41

"When Vinnie Jones and Mick Harford were in the same side you'd have needed crash helmets to play against them, never mind shin-pads.**"**

TOMMY LANGLEY

June 2002

"David broke his leg when only two while playing football, but even that didn't stop him. He was kicking the ball with his leg in plaster, and there were frequent visits to the hospital to get it re-set. **"**

VERNON LEE

father of David, whose Chelsea career was plagued by injury

❝I never got sent any knickers, but girls would write to ask where I hung out in my spare time and whether I was courting.❞

GARRY STANLEY

1970s heart-throb

❝I didn't get into girls until I was 18 because of football.**❞**

ROBERTO DI MATTEO

" The best Italian this club has signed is the chef. **"**

FRANK LEBOEUF

January 1999

**"If someone needed sorting out,
he'd do it."**

JODY MORRIS

on Dennis Wise, March 2002

❝Wisey said I think too much. But I have to do all his thinking for him.**❞**

GIANFRANCO ZOLA

May 2001

"They call me 'The Radio' because I talk. I love talking. I can't help it. It's a family problem. My wife speaks a lot. My father's always talking. Sometimes at home we need to do a time-out, like in basketball, to stop everybody from talking.**"**

GUS POYET

May 2000

"Ed de Goey is the worst-dressed man I've ever seen. One pair of jeans, one pair of trainers, one shirt and one haircut.**"**

JOHN TERRY

December 2002

❝It was a gamble to come to England but I saw what Ole Gunnar Solskjaer achieved and I thought, 'I can do better than that.'**❞**

TORE ANDRE FLO

September 1997

"Graeme Le Saux takes a lot of stick from people because he's wise, but it's just the way he is and he's a great geezer.**"**

FRANK LAMPARD

December 2002

" Quite simply, the little man is a genius. "

DENNIS WISE

on Gianfranco Zola

❝I used to share a room with Gianfranco Zola but I had to throw him out because he snored so much.**❞**

ROBERTO DI MATTEO

February 1999

If I was having a race with my mum and
I was expected to beat her by 50 yards, I'd
like to be beat her by 60 yards.
I love winning. **"**

FRANK SINCLAIR

December 1996

❝You don't get many one-club players nowadays. I definitely want to stay at Chelsea for the rest of my career.**❞**

JOHN TERRY

November 2001

❝I am sure John Terry has got a hell of a future. The only difference between him and me is that, when I tackled, they didn't get up. **❞**

RON HARRIS

May 2001

When I signed for Chelsea, all the papers made out I was an alcoholic and here for the nights out and the booze. But I'm just here to play football.

DAMIEN DUFF

October 2003

"I would be happiest, when I'm 50 or so, for people to say, 'I remember you – you were a good player.'**"**

GRAEME LE SAUX

January 1990

ffSometimes it is good to score after 43 seconds… and sometimes it is better to last a little longer.**55**

ROBERTO DI MATTEO

"I have been here since I was 14 and to be made captain of such a great team is a dream come true.**"**

JOHN TERRY

September 2004

"I think he's a fantastic captain because he's Chelsea through and through. He plays like he's got feelings for the club.**"**

Former skipper **RON "CHOPPER" HARRIS**

on John Terry, October 2004

"I know full well that I'm not a greedy person. I've not come here for money. I've come here because I want to win things and I have a good chance of winning things at Chelsea. **"**

ASHLEY COLE

signs from Arsenal, September 2006

"People will always say the best player at Chelsea has been Gianfranco Zola but I would say Peter was the greatest. He was such a strong player, a big fellow who scored goals and scared defenders.**"**

RON "CHOPPER" HARRIS

pays tribute to the late Peter Osgood, March 2006

❝I know I am not risking my life by playing again, and that is the main thing.**❞**

Brave **PETR CECH** *returns to action in January 2007, three months after a horrific head injury at Reading.*

❝If he's not the best striker in Europe, I don't know where there's a better one. His all-round game is fantastic. He's scoring spectacular goals. That's Didi and it's great to have a striker playing like that. **❞**

An excited **FRANK LAMPARD**
acknowledges Didier Drogba's scintillating form, October 2006

"Working with the humanitarian thing is something very important to me.**"**

DIDIER DROGBA

in March 2011 on his plans after retirement

❝It's an incredible achievement and my loyalty to Chelsea has paid dividends. It is a great club and I am fortunate to be the captain of a very good team.**❞**

JOHN TERRY

after leading Chelsea to four FA Cup wins, May 2012

❝He is my hero. No striker I have ever played with has scored so many important goals in finals.**❞**

FRANK LAMPARD

praises Didier Drogba after the 2012 FA Cup win

CHAPTER 3

GAFFER TALK

" My ambition is for Chelsea to set the First Division alight inside two seasons. **"**

Blues boss, **EDDIE McCREADIE**
May 1977. Two seasons later, Chelsea were relegated to the
Second Division

❝Seeing this side develop has been like planting a seed and watching it grow like a flower.**❞**

EDDIE McCREADIE

February 1977

❝I was like Red Adair, saving the team from the drop. But I knew it would only be until the end of the season.**❞**

DAVID WEBB

on his brief spell as Blues boss in 1993

"It might be poor old Chelsea,
or dear old Chelsea, but that's better
than no Chelsea at all, isn't it?**"**

Blues boss **DANNY BLANCHFLOWER**

February 1977

❝There is no club in Britain
I would rather be at. **❞**

GLENN HODDLE

April 1996, a month before he left Chelsea to
become England manager

❝I don't buy a player for his entertainment, because then you're going to work in a circus.**❞**

RUUD GULLIT

August 1997

❝Graeme Souness came in raging about a tackle by Dennis Wise on Nigel Clough. In the end I had to tell him, 'Calm down, you've just had a triple heart bypass.'**❞**

Referee **KEITH HACKETT**

November 1994

"All those bankers earning hundreds of thousands of pounds a year in the City would give it all up for 15 minutes playing for Chelsea. **"**

LAWRIE SANCHEZ

former Fulham boss

❝I think with Chris we now have what we are looking for… **❞**

GIANLUCA VIALLI

hails new signing Chris Sutton, August 1999. In the season that followed, Sutton scored one Premiership goal

**"When Ruud made it clear that
he wanted a package that would cost
us £3.7m plus bonuses we knew it was the
end of the road. "**

KEN BATES

on the sacking of Ruud Gullit, February 1998

"We had to make a change. There is no easy way to do it. Do you go for a shot in the head, or a death from a thousand cuts?**"**

KEN BATES

on the sacking of Gianluca Vialli, September 2000

" I can look back and say, 'I've lived,' and that's all down to this old funny game. **"**

GIANLUCA VIALLI

February 2000

“When I got sacked by Chelsea,
I didn't realise how much it would hurt.**”**

JOHN HOLLINS

November 1997, nine years after Ken Bates gave him his P45

❝I think Mr Ranieri will kick a few backsides, but only in a most pleasant manner.❞

RAY WILKINS

September 2000

"You may not have heard of me before I came to you last month, but I had heard of you. **"**

CLAUDIO RANIERI's

message to Chelsea fans, October 2000

" Chelsea are being managed by
Frank Spencer, the well-intentioned
but accident-prone half-wit from
Some Mothers Do 'Ave Em. **"**

The Sun's **STEVEN HOWARD**
is unimpressed with Claudio Ranieri, November 2001

"I feel very akin to the English warrior spirit – the spirit of fighting for every ball.**"**

CLAUDIO RANIERI

May 2001

"When you play every three days, the victory is a good vitamin."

CLAUDIO RANIERI

January 2002, during a busy schedule of fixtures

❝I would be disappointed if he was leaving. I have enjoyed his company in the times we meet after the game and things like that. He has a good personality and I enjoy the competition against him.**❞**

SIR ALEX FERGUSON

shows Jose Mourinho all due respect

" Chelsea deserve all the plaudits they will get and, especially on their home form, they are worthy champions. **"**

SIR ALEX FERGUSON

concedes Chelsea are worthy winners of a second successive title, April 2006

❝I am not 'the Special One'. I'm the normal one, but my wife says I am special.**❞**

Mourinho's successor **AVRAM GRANT**
makes a low-key entrance, September 2007

❝He had my full support. I'm sure two or three of the other players would say the same. **❞**

JOHN TERRY

hints at divisions in the Blues' camp after Luiz Felipe Scolari's sacking,
February 2009

❝Ballack, Cech and Drogba became my enemies. Somehow, they have a direct line to Abramovich. **❞**

LUIZ FELIPE SCOLARI

blames three senior players for his demise, February 2009

❝He was a nice guy, happy with everybody, but if you can't get the results it's difficult.**❞**

MICHAEL BALLACK

damns Scolari with faint praise, March 2009

"It's a favour for friend. Abramovich does so much for Russian football that I wanted to give something back."

Russia boss **GUUS HIDDINK**
explains why he agreed to become Chelsea's temporary manager,
February 2009

"If Mourinho is Jesus, then I am certainly not one of his apostles.**"**

New Chelsea boss **CARLO ANCELOTTI**
reveals he's not a fan of his most famous predecessor, October 2009

❝I really envy Ruud because he was so cool and calm. The way I am doing this job is a little bit different. I can't get away from thinking about football 24 hours a day.**❞**

GIANLUCA VIALLI

February 1998

❝Jose is the best in the business, there's no doubt about that, and I am sure he will be for the next 20 years. That's what we want at Chelsea, the best and only the best. **❞**

Skipper **JOHN TERRY**

wants Mourinho to stay at the Bridge

❝I don't ever remember a player playing against a side I have managed as well as he did – no matter what we did we couldn't cope with him… we tried everything but there was nothing we could do.**❞**

Sunderland boss **GUS POYET**
on Eden Hazard, 2013–14 season

" I don't know if Chelsea miss him, but we don't miss him. He did a lot of damage against us. **"**

Arsenal's **ARSENE WENGER**
is glad to see the back of Didier Drogba, September 2012

CHAPTER 4

THE SPECIAL ONE SPEAKS

❝Please don't call me arrogant, but I'm a European champion and I think I'm a special one.**❞**

JOSE MOURINHO

on his arrival at Chelsea, June 2004

❝I was not happy about these stories about me wanting an English passport and Sven's job. It was all ridiculous.**❞**

JOSE MOURINHO

rules himself out of contention to be the next England manager, October 2005

❝All of my players were magnificent and deserved to win, no doubt. We now have the first title and almost for sure we will have the second one. And that will be the big one.**❞**

JOSE MOURINHO

looks forward to more success after Chelsea's Carling Cup triumph,
February 2005

❝I think he is one of those people who is a voyeur. He likes to watch other people. There are some guys who, when they are at home, have a big telescope to see what happens in other families. He speaks, speaks, speaks about Chelsea.**❞**

JOSE MOURINHO

has a pop at Arsene Wenger, October 2005

❝I am manager today, I am the manager until the end of the season and I believe I will be the manager until the end of 2010. If I believe what I read in the press there are 11 candidates for my job but I don't get influenced by that.**❞**

JOSE MOURINHO

responds to questions about his future at Stamford Bridge,
January 2007

"My bad qualities are that I don't care about my image and because of that I don't care about the consequences of what I say and the consequences of what I do. **"**

JOSE MOURINHO

candid as ever, December 2006

109

❝It was a beautiful and rich period of my career. I want to thank all Chelsea FC supporters for what I believe is a never-ending love story.❞

JOSE MOURINHO

after he left Chelsea by "mutual consent" in September 2007

❝When I look at that team only Ivanovic and Anelka are not players from my time. So it's a team without secrets for me.**❞**

JOSE MOURINHO

claims Chelsea are still "his team" ahead of the Blues'
clash with Inter Milan, January 2010

❝This time I will go back to a different dressing room, a different dugout but I know Mourinho is normally lucky at Stamford Bridge.❞

JOSE MOURINHO

looks forward to his return to SW6 with Inter Milan,
February 2010

❝Chelsea have suffered in the last two years, and it's no coincidence that this decline happened after I left. **❞**

JOSE MOURINHO

as modest as ever, February 2010

If Roman Abramovich helped me out in training we would be bottom of the league and if I had to work in his world of big business, we would be bankrupt!

JOSE MOURINHO

during his first spell as manager

"I don't want to win the Europa League. It would be a big disappointment for me. I don't want my players to feel the Europa League is our competition.**"**

It's the Champions League or nothing for **JOSE MOURINHO**
July 2013

"He is a specialist in failure… eight years without a piece of silverware, that's failure. If I did that in Chelsea I'd leave and not come back to London.**"**

JOSE MOURINHO

blasts Arsene Wenger, February 2014

"I am not the kind of guy that makes life easy for the great players. If they are great they have to give more than the others. If they are great they cannot be happy with a few good things they do. As a manager this is the last kind of player that I praise.**"**

JOSE MOURINHO

2014

❝Boring are a team who play at home and cannot score a goal.**❞**

JOSE MOURINHO

December 2013

"When you are the type of personality that puts pressure on yourself, I don't think you need to be worried about anything else.**"**

JOSE MOURINHO

November 2013

119

❝The world has plenty of special ones –
but I was the first.**❞**

JOSE MOURINHO

November 2013

120

"We need to put the ball in the net.
Artistic football is no use without goals.**"**

JOSE MOURINHO

September 2013

CHAPTER 5

MAGIC
CHELSEA

"I was so happy to hear those Chelsea cheers. I could have wept. That wonderful crowd. They had been taking it on the chin for 50 years and always come up smiling. How well they deserved to have something to cheer about now.**"**

Captain **ROY BENTLEY**

after Chelsea's first Championship win, April 1955

❝I'd say the 1997 FA Cup Final was the highlight of my Chelsea career, just because it was such a long time since we'd won a trophy and it meant that people were talking about that team rather than previous Chelsea teams.**❞**

STEVE CLARKE

February 2002

"*Brutissimi!* Terrible! It was one of the worst games of my life!**"**

Manchester United goalkeeper **MASSIMO TAIBI**
recalls the Blues' 5–0 win in October 1999

❝Q: What time is it?
A: Five past United! **❞**

KEN BATES

cracks a joke after the same game

❝I believe the last man to score five times in a Chelsea shirt was David Mellor.**❞**

TONY BANKS MP

July 1997

❝Villa were like some two-bob team trying to get through on penalties.**❞**

KEN BATES

on the 2000 FA Cup Final, which Chelsea won 1–0

"I think Luca dropped it, and then tried to blame it on me! I'm not quite sure who dropped it, actually. It wasn't me, honest! **"**

DENNIS WISE

explains a dent in the lid of the FA Cup, November 2000

"Yoghurts are down at Asda.**"**

GRAEME LE SAUX

when asked for his "Save of the Month", September 1998

❝ The appointment of Jose Mourinho is all about building on the foundations which we have already established at Chelsea. His record of sustained success makes him perfect for what we want to achieve. **❞**

Chelsea chief executive **PETER KENYON**

June 2004

❝The day at Bolton when we won the League will always be special, but to get my hands on the trophy at Charlton and lift it, it was the best thing in my life so far. **❞**

JOHN TERRY

reflects on Chelsea's Premier League title triumph, September 2005

❝It's a massive achievement. United have dominated this league for a while, but now we're putting down our marker and proving that we're capable of doing that.**❞**

JOE COLE

relishes Chelsea's second Premier League title, 2006

❝Stand up for the special one.**❞**

CHELSEA FANS

chant in appreciation of Jose Mourinho

"He simply was the most successful Chelsea manager ever, and the best manager I have ever worked with.**"**

JOHN TERRY

pays tribute to Jose Mourinho, September 2007

❝It was one of the biggest achievements of my career, winning in the Mecca of world football.**❞**

GUUS HIDDINK

signs off his brief stint as Blues boss with victory in the FA Cup Final against Everton at Wembley, May 2009

❝It's quite a unique situation to win as a player and to be able to coach the team and win it as well, so I feel honoured to have this chance.**❞**

ROBERTO DI MATTEO

after winning the 2012 FA Cup as manager

ᴌᴌIt's an incredible achievement by this group of players. A lot of people had written us off but we showed again what kind of character these players have.**ᴊᴊ**

ROBERTO DI MATTEO

after beating Barcelona to reach the final of the
2012 UEFA Champions League

“This is right up there, the way we've finished the season in such style. We deserved to come out on top. The first two titles we won relatively easily. They were very special because they were the first ones, but with the difficulties we've had this year, that was very, very special.**”**

FRANK LAMPARD

on the 2009–10 Premier League title, May 2010

❝It was written a long time ago that Chelsea were going to win. The cup is going back to Stamford Bridge and it is the best feeling ever.**❞**

DIDIER DROGBA

after winning the 2012 UEFA Champions League

" They're crying. It was Drogba, it was the angels, it was the heavens, it was the stars, it was the gods, it was everything for Chelsea. This is not anything to do with football. This is more than football, this is spirit. Never giving in, fighting to the end, that English spirit running right the way through this Champions League for Chelsea. **"**

GARY NEVILLE's

punditry after Chelsea won the
2012 UEFA Champions League Final

" This feels magnificent. It's been three hard years seeing Manchester United lift it. We've got it back now and we need to do what United have done and maintain this success for a few years. **"**

JOHN TERRY

after winning the 2009–10 Premier League title

CHAPTER 6

IT'S GREAT TO BE A BLUE

" I've played for some big clubs
but Chelsea were the tops.
I loved the place, still do. **"**

MICKEY THOMAS

"I would love to relive those days at Chelsea – they were wonderful times. **"**

JIMMY GREAVES

Chelsea has always been my first love. I'd have liked to have spent the whole of my career at Stamford Bridge, but it was not to be. I always have a special place in my football heart for Chelsea.

TERRY VENABLES

January 1991

“The Chelsea goal-posts have become my friends, next to all the fellows who have been my team-mates over the years.**”**

PETER BONETTI

April 1976

❝We remember Peter as one of Chelsea's most skilful, yet modest, players, a model professional and a wonderful club man.**❞**

CHELSEA PROGRAMME

tribute to Peter Houseman, who died in a car crash, March 1977

❝ Somehow it's always a better feeling when you put one in at the Shed end – you get such a roar from those fans. **❞**

CLIVE WALKER

October 1978

The local TV station asked me how it felt to be joining Southampton. I said, 'To be honest, I might be wearing this Southampton shirt, but I still feel like a Chelsea player.' As you can imagine, that went down like a lead balloon.

KEN MONKOU

on leaving Chelsea in August 1992

"Chelsea play in white socks. I always win things in white socks.**"**

RUUD GULLIT

July 1995

"My biggest regret is that I never won anything at Stamford Bridge. I loved the club and still do.**"**

CLIVE WALKER

December 1994

"Every time I see him it reminds me to buy a pint of milk on the way home.**"**

Chelsea kitman **AARON LINCOLN**

on Mikael Forssell's pale features

"It was laughable, no? I mean, how can the captain of Chelsea, in the middle of the season, leave the club? To go to Manchester? I mean, it's not possible...**"**

MARCEL DESAILLY

on a rumoured move to Manchester United, April 2002

❝I played for Napoli and it was blue.
I play for Chelsea and it's blue. Italy is blue.
Blue belongs to me, my life.**❞**

GIANFRANCO ZOLA

January 2002

" Everybody is talking about Chelsea. Real Madrid is no different to anyone. There's lots of interest. Everybody is talking about the ambition of the London club, Chelsea. **"**

CLAUDE MAKELELE

September 2003

" The Chelsea Mourinho is the same guy as the Porto Mourinho. You have to prove youself in every training session, to demand more of yourself the whole time. **"**

PAULO FERREIRA

who played under Mourinho at Porto before Chelsea, October 2005

"On paper we've got the best squad around, best manager and we're hungrier than anyone else. Put those three together and you'll never be far off.**"**

DAMIEN DUFF

anticipates more success, September 2005

❝ Roman Abramovich is turning Chelsea into one of Europe's elite clubs, and I think it's a great thing. The fans are getting to see great players and that's what it's all about. ❞

Former **SOCCER AM** *presenter and Chelsea fan* **TIM LOVEJOY**
December 2004

"We are like soldiers going out to perform our duty. It is a big battle ahead and we have to conquer the enemy to move forward and succeed. **"**

MICHAEL ESSIEN

declares war on title rivals Manchester United, December 2006

❝I hope the club can help me fulfil my ambition to become one of the top players in the world. I really wanted to be a Chelsea player. Finally, I got it right.**❞**

JOHN OBI MIKEL

joins Chelsea after a protracted transfer saga, August 2006

"The fans are awesome, every player wants to play in a place where he is fully accepted and I've that here at Chelsea.**"**

A contented **DIDIER DROGBA**

November 2006

❝I do not know if he is a referee or a thief. There are no words to describe the person who was on the pitch there. **❞**

JOSE BOSINGWA

is unimpressed by Norwegian ref Tom Henning Ovrebo's performance in the Chelsea–Barcelona Champions League semi-final, May 2009

IT'S GREAT TO BE A BLUE

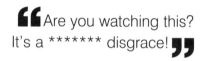Are you watching this?
It's a ******* disgrace!

An emotional **DIDIER DROGBA**

swears on live TV, at the end of the same match

"It's a load of crap and you can quote me on that.**"**

UEFA General Secretary **DAVID TAYLOR**
*bluntly dismisses talk of an anti-Chelsea conspiracy after the
Blues' controversial defeat by Barcelona, May 2009*

"I love this club. Those last eight years have been the best in my career and in my entire life.**"**

DIDIER DROGBA

May 2012

> **"** That's the reason why I came here, to win trophies and to make history with the club. The result is great for us, for the fans, the club. Our fourth FA Cup final, fourth win, fourth trophy. **"**

DIDIER DROGBA

after the 2012 FA Cup win

"You talk about the Zolas and the best players to have played at the club, but for me he [Lampard] is the best.**"**

JOHN TERRY

praises Frank Lampard's 200-goal tally

" Farewell Didier Drogba. You have enthralled us, occasionally enraged us, but always entertained us. A striking superstar. **"**

GARY LINEKER

on Twitter, May 2012

" This is a very significant day for Chelsea, capturing one of the best players in the world with his peak years ahead of him. I hope every Chelsea fan is as excited as I am with this news. **"**

Chairman **BRUCE BUCK**

after buying Fernando Torres, January 2011

❝It's my dream to win the
Champions League and I'm sure I can,
playing for Chelsea. **❞**

FERNANDO TORRES

January 2011

173

CHAPTER 7

CELEBRITY VIEWS

"Chelsea were the natural team for me to support. I would catch the 45 bus from Loughborough Junction to Battersea Bridge, and then walk across the bridge. I'd supported them earlier, but I actually started going in the year they won the Championship, 1954–55.**"**

JOHN MAJOR

August 1990

❝I played against Ron Harris and he frightened the life out of me. Thankfully, he never whacked me, and I appreciate that. **❞**

Former Tottenham winger **PETER TAYLOR**

❝Skilful as he was, Ossie could dish it out and I was no shrinking violet. We hated each other with venom.**❞**

FRANK McLINTOCK

captain of Arsenal's 1971 Double-winning team

"What they say about footballers being ignorant is rubbish. I spoke to a couple yesterday and they were quite intelligent.**"**

RAQUEL WELCH

after a visit to the Bridge in 1973

❝Hoddle was one of my idols
and it would have been brilliant to
link up with the likes of Ruud Gullit,
Dennis Wise and Mark Hughes. **❞**

IAN WRIGHT

on a never-to-happen move to West London

❝I had a lot of offers but Chelsea were the only club I would have signed for. **❞**

GEORGE BEST

(sadly the Blues couldn't afford his wage demands)

❝Dad supported Arsenal but I was a Chelsea fan. I'll never forget the first game I saw. It was Chelsea at home to West Ham, and I remember Clive Walker was in the side. He was a player who excited me, and I couldn't wait to go back.**❞**

PAUL MERSON

1995

"I was a Chelsea fanatic. When my turn to choose the bedroom décor coincided with their FA Cup-winning run of 1970, I gave Mum a Chelsea rosette so she could buy the wallpaper and bed covers in exactly the right colours.**"**

IAN BOTHAM

1994

❝I actually don't look forward to Chelsea games these days because they've become real wars.**❞**

TOM "LOFTY" WATT

writer, actor and Arsenal fan

"There's only one real Chelsea kit – the classic kit of the early 70s. The worst has to be the tangerine and grey. What the hell's that got to do with Chelsea?**"**

TIM LOVEJOY

TV presenter

❝I think we were meant to be in a state of continual frustration. I think it might upset everyone more than they know if we actually won something.**❞**

DAVID BADDIEL

September 1995

❝Wisey would have made it as a scrum-half. He would have adapted and the game would have knocked that edge out of him. **❞**

England rugby international **BRIAN MOORE**

❝The fastest man at Stamford Bridge was Clive Walker. I raced him in a 60-metres dash. I won't tell you who won, but we were both dipping for the tape.**❞**

SEB COE

April 1991

❝I've asked John Major if he's going to start coming again. He gets a bloody good pension as a former prime minister, so he might even be able to afford a season ticket.**❞**

TONY BANKS MP

July 1997

" When I was at school, I preferred football to cricket. Until cricket took over, I'd play football on Saturday mornings and then go to watch Chelsea in the afternoons, standing in the Shed. **"**

ALEC STEWART

September 1990

❝I don't like to lump Chelsea in
with all the other London clubs.
They are too individualistic for that.
Middlesex has been Chelsea's county since
AD 703 and that's how I like to think of them,
a Middlesex club.**❞**

Astrologer **RUSSELL GRANT**

September 1990

191

> **"** He's not running for Pope or sainthood;
> he's a footballer. **"**

Respect MP **GEORGE GALLOWAY**

defends John Terry on BBC's Question Time, *February 2010*